1919–
1994
HARCOURT BRACE & COMPANY
SEVENTY-FIVE YEARS

D1013638

A WEDDING IN HELL

CHARLES SIMIC

A WEDDING
IN HELL

POEMS

A Harvest Original
Harcourt Brace & Company
San Diego   New York   London

RO123294474
HUMCA

HOUSTON PUBLIC LIBRARY

Copyright © 1994 by Charles Simic

All rights reserved. No part of this publication may be reproduced or trans-
mitted in any form or by any means, electronic or mechanical, including
photocopy, recording, or any information storage and retrieval system, without
permission in writing from the publisher.

Requests for permission to make copies of any part of the work should be
mailed to: Permissions Department, Harcourt Brace & Company, 6277 Sea
Harbor Drive, Orlando, Florida 32887-6777.

Some of these poems first appeared, often in different versions and under
different titles, in the following magazines, to whose editors grateful acknowl-
edgment is made: *The New Yorker, The Southern Review, The Yale Review,
The Nation, Colorado Review, Agni Review, Another Chicago Magazine, New
American Writing, Poetry, Harvard Review, Field, Michigan Quarterly Review,
Mudfish, The Prose Poem, The Georgia Review, Boulevard,* and *The Gettysburg
Review.*

Library of Congress Cataloging-in-Publication Data
Simic, Charles, 1938–
    A wedding in hell: poems/Charles Simic.—1st ed.
      p.   cm.
    ISBN 0-15-100123-5 (hardcover).—ISBN 0-15-600129-2 (pbk.)
    I. Title.
  PS3569.I4725W43   1994
  811'.54—dc20   94-11941

The text was set in Granjon.
Based on a design by Lydia D'moch
Printed in the United States of America
First edition
A B C D E

In memory of my mother

CONTENTS

ONE

TWO

ONE

MIRACLE GLASS CO.

Heavy mirror carried
Across the street,
I bow to you
And to everything that appears in you,
Momentarily
And never again the same way:

This street with its pink sky,
Row of gray tenements,
A lone dog,
Children on rollerskates,
Woman buying flowers,
Someone looking lost.

In you, mirror framed in gold
And carried across the street
By someone I can't even see,
To whom, too, I bow.

LATE ARRIVAL

The world was already here,
Serene in its otherness.
It only took you to arrive
On the late afternoon train
To where no one awaited you.

A town no one ever remembered
Because of its drabness,
Where you lost your way
Searching for a place to stay
In a maze of identical streets.

It was then that you heard,
As if for the very first time,
The sound of your own footsteps
Under a church clock
Which had stopped just as you did

Between two empty streets
Aglow in the afternoon sunlight,
Two modest stretches of infinity
For you to wonder at
Before resuming your walk.

CHILDHOOD AT THE MOVIES

We were waiting for the monster.
Time passed slowly in the dark forest.
The lone rider on the prairie
Made my heart leap with joy.
I lived in the clouds; I was learning to fly.

A storm was brewing; the moon kept vanishing.
I followed a man in a black overcoat
Who carried an empty coffin over his shoulder.
The trees were haunted and so was the house.
The crows on the highway were like wind-up toys.

The sailor on the river barge played the accordion.
The woman in a transparent nightgown looked at me.
How long ago it all was!
We were waiting for the monster, hunched in our seats
As if trying to deflect blows.

The mechanical chess player wore a red turban.
The evening was warm, the windows were open.
The scorpion crawled on a child's sleeping face,
But when we went to look with eyes full of fear,
There was only the sea and sky everywhere.

TATTOOED CITY

I, who am only an incomprehensible
Bit of scribble
On some warehouse wall
Or some subway entrance.

Matchstick figure,
Heart pierced by arrow,
Scratch of a meter maid
On a parked hearse.

CRAZY CHARLIE in red spraypaint
Crowding for warmth
With other unknown divinities
In an underpass at night.

DREAM AVENUE

Monumental, millennial decrepitude,
As tragedy requires. A broad
Avenue with trash unswept,
A few solitary speck-sized figures
Going about their business
In a world already smudged by a schoolboy's eraser.

You've no idea what city this is,
What country? It could be a dream,
But is it yours? You're nothing
But a vague sense of loss,
A piercing, heart-wrenching dread
On an avenue with no name

With a few figures conveniently small
And blurred who in any case
Have their backs to you
As they look elsewhere, beyond
The long row of gray buildings and their many windows,
Some of which appear broken.

SINISTER COMPANY

Just the other day
On the busy street
You stopped to search your pockets
For some change
When you noticed them following you:

Blind, deaf, mad, and homeless,
Out of respect keeping their distance.
You are our King! they shouted.
Chief headsman!
The world's greatest lion tamer!

As for your pockets,
There was a hole in each one.
At which they drew close,
Touching you everywhere,
Raising a paper crown to your head.

HAUNTED MIND

Savageries to come,
Cities smelling of death already,
What idol will you worship,
Whose icy heart?

One cold Thursday night,
In a neighborhood dive,
I watched the Beast of War
Lick its sex on TV.

There were three other customers:
Mary sitting in old Joe's lap,
Her crazy son in the corner
With arms spread wide over the pinball machine.

PARADISE MOTEL

Millions were dead; everybody was innocent.
I stayed in my room. The President
Spoke of war as of a magic love potion.
My eyes were opened in astonishment.
In a mirror my face appeared to me
Like a twice–canceled postage stamp.

I lived well, but life was awful.
There were so many soldiers that day,
So many refugees crowding the roads.
Naturally, they all vanished
With a touch of the hand.
History licked the corners of its bloody mouth.

On the pay channel, a man and a woman
Were trading hungry kisses and tearing off
Each other's clothes while I looked on
With the sound off and the room dark
Except for the screen where the color
Had too much red in it, too much pink.

ON A SIDE STREET

If there are small shops
With illegible signs,
Don't come near them
Or look in their windows.

Keep to where the sky can be seen
In its cloudless twilight splendor
Above the dark buildings,
Dark even on darkest nights.
If someone's following you,
And he limps, and he's got a watch
He puts to his ear smiling,
Run from him and his watch.

There's a wide, well-lit avenue
Close by. Thousands have come out
Just to see you, though
They make believe you're invisible
As you step into the light
Out of that dark side street,
With your face so pale
It seems powdered for a carnival.

Mr. Zoo Keeper, will you be making your rounds today? We are howling, we are clucking in distress. It's been ages since you came. We smell awful, we smell to high heaven. Sorrow, sickness, and fleabites are our lot.

The rabbits still screw but their weakness is optimism. Even the lion doesn't believe the fables anymore. "Pray to the Lord," the monkeys shriek.

I've dyed my hair green like Baudelaire. The big circus tent, I tell everybody, still stands in the distance. I can see the trumpets glow. I can hear the snare drum.

Ours is a circus of quick, terrified glances.

A WEDDING IN HELL

They were pale like the stones on the meadow
The black sheep lick.
Pale stones like children in their Sunday clothes
Playing at bride and groom.

There we found a clock face with Roman numerals
In the old man's overcoat pocket.
He kept looking at the sky without recognizing it,
And now it was time for a little rain to fall.

Your sheltering hands, Mother, which made the old man
    disappear.
The Lord who saw over them
Saw into our hearts while we unlaced his boots.

I'm turning off the lights so His eyes won't find you,
    you said.
O dreams like evening shadows on a windy meadow,
And your hands, Mother, like white mice.

THE DEAD IN PHOTOGRAPHS

They were all mere beginners.
They stood still for the camera,
Only a few thinking to move
And make a blur at the right moment.

Others held their smiles seemingly forever.
It was their wedding day.
Here they were by the side of the road
On the way to California.
The groom had a wide tie on with green parrots.
The bride wore a straw hat
With a topping of strawberries.

In Los Angeles it was Sunday morning.
The photographer took a picture
Of a closed barber shop,
A black cat crossing an empty avenue,
A tall palm tree in the wind.

Then the dead reappeared.
A blind man stood on a street corner
Playing the guitar and singing.
The little boy walked up to the camera
And stuck out his tongue at us.

MADAME THEBES

That awful deceit of appearances.
Some days
Everything looks unfamiliar
On my street.
It's somebody else's life I'm living.

An immaculate silent order
Of white buildings and dark clouds,
And then the open door
In a house with lowered voices.
Someone left in a hurry,
And they're waiting for me to come in
With a lit match.

There's a rustle of a long skirt,
But when I enter
It's only the evening papers
Sliding off the table
Bird-like
In a large and drafty
And now altogether empty room.

DOCUMENTARY

Today I saw a city burning on TV.
Someone distant and ghostlike
Walked through the rubble,
And then the camera made a sweep
Of the fiery sky and the clouds.

Alone, stepping carefully,
His head bowed so low—he didn't have a head—
While searching for something
Of no interest to the camera
Which wanted us to admire the sky
With its towers of black smoke,

And the accompanying commentary,
Words about "our tragic age,"
Which I didn't hear—watching him
Stop and bend over
Just as he vanished from view.

EVENING VISITOR

You remind me of those dwarfs in Velázquez.
Former dogcatcher
Promoted to professor at a correspondence school
With a matchbook address.

That couple screwing and watching
Themselves in the mirror,
Do you approve of them
As they gasp and roll their eyes in ecstasy?

And how about the solitary wine drinker?
He's drinking because he can't decide
Whether to kill only one of them or both—
And here it's already morning!

Some damn bird chirping in the trees.
Is that it? I beseech you. Answer me!

THE OLDEST CHILD

The night still frightens you.
You know it is interminable
And of vast, unimaginable dimensions.
"That's because His insomnia is permanent,"
You've read some mystic say.
Is it the point of His schoolboy's compass
That pricks your heart?

Somewhere perhaps the lovers lie
Under the dark cypress trees,
Trembling with happiness,
But here there's only your beard of many days
And a night moth shivering
Under your hand pressed against your chest.

Oldest child, Prometheus
Of some cold, cold fire you can't even name
For which you're serving slow time
With that night moth's terror for company.

THE MASSACRE OF THE INNOCENTS

The poets of the Late Tang Dynasty
Could do nothing about it except to write:
"On the western hills the sun sets . . .
Horses blown by the whirlwind tread the clouds."

I could not help myself either. I felt joy
Even at the sight of a crow circling
As I stretched out on the grass
Alone now with the silence of the sky.

Only the wind making a slight rustle
As it turned the pages of the book by my side,
Back and forth, searching for something
For that bloody crow to read.

PASCAL'S IDEA

My insignificance is a sign of my greatness.
Marvel, draw back
As I scurry in my roachlike way
Through these greasy kitchens
With their raised knives
And their fat-assed cooks
Bent over steaming pots.

My life is a triumph over the world's connivances
And blind chance.
I found the poison you left for me
Extremely nourishing.

Once I sipped milk out of a saucer left for the cat.
Once I ran across a birthday cake
With its candles already lit.
It was terrifying
And I suppose a bit like
What your heaven and hell combined must be.

THE WORLD

You who torture me
Every day
With your many cruel instruments,
I'm about to confess to
A despair
Darker than all your darkest
Nights.

The day you brought me
A picture of a woman
And a child fleeing
On a road lined with trees,
And another of the same two
Now fallen
With bloodied heads
On that same winding road

With its cloudless sky
Of late summer
And its trees shivering
In the first cool breeze
On days when we put all
Our trust into the world
Only to be deceived.

THE CLOCKS OF THE DEAD

One night I went to keep the clock company.
It had a loud tick after midnight
As if it were uncommonly afraid.
It's like whistling past a graveyard,
I explained.
In any case, I told him I understood.

Once there were clocks like that
In every kitchen in America.
Now the factory's windows are all broken.
The old men on night shift are in Charon's boat.
The day you stop, I said to the clock,
The little wheels they keep in reserve
Will have rolled away
Into many hard-to-find places.

Just thinking about it, I forgot to wind the clock.
We woke up in the dark.
How quiet the city is, I said.
Like the clocks of the dead, my wife replied.
Grandmother on the wall,
I heard the snows of your childhood
Begin to fall.

RASKOLNIKOV

Philosophical murderer, times are propitious
For your edifying experiments.
Even in the sunlight the world looks evil.
Every building on every street
Has most of its windows boarded up.
With a hard smile the old woman pushes
Her shopping cart slowly through the rubble,

Men and women—sleeping five or six to a room—
Who have come to such despair,
Words fail them. They are beyond remedy
And therefore not to be talked about.
And yet, there he is in the playground
Pint in hand, peeing in silence
In full view of the elevated train.

He is as real as he is expendable,
Says someone who'd like to stir things up a bit.
The weather's hot. Every night the crowd's
In a foul mood roaming the streets late,
Their hearts already consenting secretly.

In the meantime, is he the one with the clipped skull
Talking to himself? Or the one
With the Seeing Eye dog and the white cane?
Or perhaps the one in the policeman's uniform
Speeding through the red light?

TWO

No lack of customers, I assure you. We have Cain and his brother to rent. The knife costs extra. The soldiers from the siege of Stalingrad are still wrapped in rags and frozen in the snow.

We carry the matches that set fire to Atlanta, the rope with which Ulysses tied himself to the mast to listen to the sirens. Here's Pascal's watch. It's as silent as your soul. And there, the sky made darker by unanswered prayers to cover yourself with on a night like this.

For that naked, long-haired saint hiding in the shadows, you'll want to construct a screeching pulley. His eyes will roll, his groans will delight you.

Cleopatra's cat, do we have Cleopatra's cat? she asks.

THIS MORNING

Enter without knocking, hard-working ant.
I'm just sitting here mulling over
What to do this dark, overcast day.
It was a night of the radio turned low,
Fitful sleep, vague, troubling dreams.
I woke up lovesick and confused.
I thought I heard Estella in the garden singing
And some bird answering her,
But it was the rain. Dark treetops swaying
And whispering. "Come to me, my desire,"
I said. And she came to me by and by,
Her breath smelling of mint, her tongue
Wetting my cheek, and then she vanished.
Slowly day came, a gray streak of daylight
To bathe my hands and face in.
Hours passed, and then you crawled
Under the door, and stopped before me.
You visit the same tailors the mourners do,
Mr. Ant. I like the silence between us,
The quiet—that holy state even the rain
Knows about. Listen to her begin to fall,
As if with eyes closed,
Muting each drop in her wild-beating heart.

THE CHURCH OF INSOMNIA

The huge congregation is in the dark. The altar is a bed with a canopy. The minister reads by candlelight the works of Jonathan Edwards. If you listen hard you'll hear pages being turned, the ash of his cigarette fall into the abyss.

The cat with the mouse in its mouth is merely passing through.

HEROIC MOMENT

I went bare-assed into the battle. The President himself heard of my insolence. I was given a flea-bitten mutt to ride. I rode in the company of crows with a red plastic pisspot on my head and a dollhouse knife between my teeth.

When she heard the news, my mother caused the Greek fleet to be deprived of favorable winds on its way to Troy. Witch, they called her, dirty witch—and she, so pretty, chopping the mushrooms, laughing and crying over the stew pot.

THE BEGGAR ON HOUSTON STREET

He was like Spider Man,
He tells me.
The way he climbed burning buildings
With a fireman's ax.

Gene Tierney, what ever
Happened to her? he asks.
Now, there was fire
To steal from the gods!

Back then they held cockfights
On tenement roofs.
The feathers flew high,
And then drifted on the wind.

The sunset today confirms it.
The laundry on the line
Like red flags flying
In the battle of Catalonia.

And in the movies then—
Dark and so crowded,
You could barely find a seat
To see her play Laura.

Beauty is always dying, he sighs.
She, if he remembers correctly,
Didn't appear to be in the least
Surprised about that.

WANTED POSTER

From the closed, block-long post office
I heard him whisper
Out of his flyspecked mouth
As I hurried by on the street.
Hunted beast, he said.
With eyes dark and mean under the rusty thumbtacks,
Who furloughed you today
To go around grinning at every woman you meet?

HAPPINESS

Do not flatter yourself,
It's just the open window,
A bird singing,
The bright sunlight.

The hundred-year-old woman in a dream
Closed the door ever so softly,
And still you woke with a start
To the trees full of leaves
Not a single one of which was moving.

There was a dead child in her arms.
Over her shoulder a city on fire
As if after an air raid.
A whiff of putrefaction reached your nostrils

In this enchanted place,
With its blue sky,
Trees like a mystery religion,
A lost ant going the wrong way, perhaps,
Under your black shoe?

EXPLAINING A FEW THINGS

Every worm is a martyr,
Every sparrow subject to injustice,
I said to my cat,
Since there was no one else around.

It's raining. In spite of their huge armies
What can the ants do?
And the roach on the wall
Like a waiter in an empty restaurant?

I'm going in the cellar
To stroke the rat caught in a trap.
You watch the sky.
If it clears, scratch on the door.

GRIM CONTINGENCIES

If the wicked didn't get such kicks
Out of doing evil, ladies,
These cherries would taste even sweeter,
Plato and Emerson would suffice,
And the sight of Miss Angela
Soaping her breasts in the cold lake
Would be all we need of paradise.

Women understand that. The blue sky,
The sweet breeze that came to make us amorous,
That's just the world's oldest bluff.
While we were rolling in the hay,
They were scheming how to squeeze us,
Between their long dirty nails, like bedbugs.

Besides, one is always speaking from
Underneath a pile of fresh corpses.
Is that so? Yes, my dream girls.
Even while imbibing too many Bloody Marys
Before lunch, even while doddering
Like an old bumblebee from flower to flower
Making everybody howl with laughter . . .

THE CRYSTAL PYRAMID

It's not by the river Nile; it's on the kitchen table attracting cosmic forces. My sorceress, is what I call her! Her breasts are naked as she mutters over it with eyes tightly shut. My name is Rat Amor because I have a good little line of talk and because my soul sleeps in a cellar.

The knives are being sharpened and her long nails, too, with which she brushes one cheek, and then the other. The pyramid is drawing blood. A red mask from a queen's tomb on her face and my picture on the floor, greasy whiskers and all, under her spiked heel.

POCKET THEATER

Fingers in an overcoat pocket. Fingers sticking out of a black leather glove. The nails chewed raw. One play is called "Thieves' Market," another "Night in a Dime Museum." The fingers when they strip are like bewitching nude bathers or the fake wooden limbs in a cripple factory. No one ever sees the play: you put your hand in somebody else's pocket on the street and feel the action.

DIVINE COLLABORATOR

He's the silent partner of everything we write; the father of all language out of silence.

Cuss or pray all you want! He owns every one of our words and is only lending them to us, even when we write to the one we love madly, saying:

"My dearest, you must understand my back hurts, I could not get out of bed. I lay there all day listening to the rain and dreaming of you aroused by my caresses, offering your naked thighs to me . . .

"Disgusting pig, you must be thinking as you read this! Remember, love,

this is God writing!"

THE SUPREME MOMENT

As an ant is powerless
Against a raised boot,
And only has an instant
To have a bright idea or two.
The black boot so polished,
He can see himself
Reflected in it, distorted,
Perhaps made larger
Into a huge monster ant
Shaking his arms and legs
Threateningly?

The boot may be hesitating,
Demurring, having misgivings,
Gathering cobwebs,
Dew?
Yes, and apparently no.

CRAZY ABOUT HER SHRIMP

We don't even take time
To come up for air.
We keep our mouths full and busy
Eating bread and cheese
And smooching in between.

No sooner have we made love
Than we are back in the kitchen.
While I chop the hot peppers,
She wiggles her ass
And stirs the shrimp on the stove.

How good the wine tastes
That has run red
Out of a laughing mouth!
Down her chin
And onto her naked tits.

"I'm getting fat," she says,
Turning this way and that way
Before the mirror.
"I'm crazy about her shrimp!"
I shout to the gods above.

TRANSPORT

In the frying pan
On the stove
I found my love
And me naked.

Chopped onions
Fell on our heads
And made us cry.
It's like a parade,
I told her, confetti
When some guy
Reaches the moon.

"Means of transport,"
She replied obscurely
While we fried.
"Means of transport!"

AWAITING JUDGEMENT

I threw myself on the mercy of the court.
Everything had grown silent:
The midnight sky, the village dogs,
The trees which only a moment ago were agitated
For a reason known only to themselves.

My judge had disappeared.
Then in a lit upstairs window
I saw her gloriously undressed for bed.
My defender, too, had walked off.
I saw the light of her cigarette
At the end of the driveway,
And then all was shadow and danger.

I knelt in the grass,
Admiring the majesty of the sky,
The magnitude of its indifference
Above the leaves beginning to stir again
As if at the sight of quickly built gallows.

LOVE FLEA

He took a flea
From her armpit
To keep

And cherish
In a matchbox,
Even pricking his finger

From time to time
To feed it
Drops of blood.

WHAT I OVERHEARD

In summer's idle time,
When trees grow heavy with leaves
And spread shade everywhere
That is a delight to lie in
Alone
Or in the company of a dear friend,

Dreaming or having a quiet talk
Without looking at each other,
Until she feels drowsy
As if after too much wine,
And you draw close for a kiss
On her cheek, and instead
Stay with lips pursed, listening

To a bee make its rounds lazily,
And a far-off rooster crow
On the edge of sleep with the leaves hushed
Or rustling, ever so softly,
About something or other on their mind.

THE SECRET

Blue jays screeching
Early
About some intruder
In the yard.

You had to slip naked
Out of bed
To peek
Once, twice
Out of the window,
And then tiptoe
Quickly
Out of the room
And down the stairs.

I thought I heard
The screen door
Softly shut
And then I thought I didn't,

Sweet tiptoer.

LEAVES

Lovers who take pleasure
In the company of trees,
Who seek diversion after many kisses
In each other's arms,
Watching the leaves,

The way they quiver
At the slightest breath of wind,
The way they thrill,
And shudder almost individually,
One of them beginning to shake
While the others are still quiet,
Unaccountably, unreasonably—

What am I saying?
One leaf in a million more fearful,
More happy,
Than all the others?

On this oak tree casting
Such deep shade,
And my lids closing sleepily
With that one leaf twittering
Now darkly, now luminously.

THREE

THE PLEASURES OF READING

On his deathbed my father is reading
The memoirs of Casanova.
I'm watching the night fall,
A few windows being lit across the street.
In one of them a young woman is reading
Close to the glass.
She hasn't looked up in a long while,
Even with the darkness coming.

While there's still a bit of light,
I want her to lift her head,
So I can see her face
Which I have already imagined,
But her book must be full of suspense.
And besides, it's so quiet,
Every time she turns a page,
I can hear my father turn one too,
As if they are reading the same book.

IN ECSTASY OF SURRENDER

My father steps out
Into the vanishing point.
He dwindles. He is tiny.
He can't help himself.
It takes me a long time
To find him again.
I need a sharp pencil,
And then, all of a sudden,
I need an eyelash
To point with.

There where the lines draw close,
So alike, so severe,
I've never seen anything like it!
He almost gone,
Emptying away.
A kind of groping it was,
Yes, a groping
While remaining stock-still,

And I, of course,
Wanting to follow
After him,
While being unwilling to
Just then.

WHERE THE DREAMY WABASH FLOWS

A world's disappearing.
Little street,
You were too narrow,
Too much in the shade already.

You had only one dog,
One lone child.
You hid your biggest mirror,
Your undressed lovers.

Someone carted them off
In an open truck.
They were still embraced traveling
On their sofa

Over a darkening plain,
Some unknown Kansas or Nebraska
With a storm brewing.
The woman opening a red umbrella

In the truck. The boy
And the dog running after them,
As if after a rooster
With its head chopped off.

A PUPPET PLAY

The fly in it is the only living creature. The puppets run after it, construct various kinds of traps, and in the end catch it. They pluck its wings and remove its legs one by one. A girl holds a burning match over the shuddering insect. "O fly, don't you know it's much worse to die alone in some crack in the wall," she chants.

What excitement! A boy with glasses runs on the stage gesticulating wildly. He has brought the world's smallest wheelchair for the fly. There's even a tiny American flag, a tin cup, and a trumpet which is unfortunately too big to fit in its mouth.

HOARDER OF TRAGEDY

With the stench of war in the air,
He takes the old baby carriage.
Some of it he carts that way,
Some of it he stuffs in his raincoat pockets.

Sunset comes to blind his eyes,
As he surveys the piles of newspapers
In his bedroom and kitchen,
The yellowed embankments and towers
With their screaming headlines,

Waiting for him to kneel before them,
Saying, have pity on me my hoard,
Don't crush me as I sleep
Fitfully and with many mysterious
Awakenings and sittings up in bed.

PAPER DOLLS CUT OUT OF A NEWSPAPER

Four of them holding hands like a family.
There's a war on this morning
And an advertisement for heavenly coffee
Next to a picture of a murderer.

Hold them up, little Rosie.
Hold them up a bit longer.
Watch them dance, watch them shake
And make us laugh.

The coffee is boiling, its steam
Rises. The printer's ink comes off
On your fingers, on your face
When you cover your eyes, Rosie.

READING HISTORY

for Hans Magnus

At times, reading here
In the library,
I'm given a glimpse
Of those condemned to death
Centuries ago,
And of their executioners.
I see each pale face before me
The way a judge
Pronouncing a sentence would,
Marveling at the thought
That I do not exist yet.

With eyes closed I can hear
The evening birds.
Soon they will be quiet
And the final night on earth
Will commence
In the fullness of its sorrow.

How vast, dark, and impenetrable
Are the early morning skies
Of those led to their death
In a world from which I'm entirely absent,
Where I can still watch
Someone's slumped back,

Someone who is walking away from me
With his hands tied,
His graying head still on his shoulders,

Someone who
In what little remains of his life
Knows in some vague way about me,
And thinks of me as God,
As Devil.

MEN DEIFIED BECAUSE OF THEIR CRUELTY

Is it true tyrants have long fingers?
Is it true that they set their own traps
Beneath paintings of the Madonna
In gloomy palaces turned into museums?

We all love her feverish eyes raised to heaven.
We all love the naked Venus too.
She's watching us from an unmade bed
With a smile and her hand on her crotch.

She can see the master lurk behind our backs.
He's old, he's cadaverous, he is dressed
As a museum guard, and he wears gray gloves,
Because, of course, his hands are red.

PSALM

You've been a long time making up your mind,
O Lord, about these madmen
Running the world. Their reach is long
And their claws must have frightened you.

One of them found me with his shadow.
The day turned chill. I dangled
Between terror and valor
In the darkest corner of my son's bedroom.

I sought with my eyes, You in whom I do not believe.
You've been busy making the flowers pretty,
The lambs run after their mother,
Or perhaps you haven't been doing even that?

It was spring. The killers were full of sport
And merriment, and your divines
Were right at their side, to make sure
Our final goodbyes were said properly.

THE STORY OF CERCOPES
after Ovid

For once the father of the gods, thoroughly disgusted
By the deceitful, Bible-thumping Cercopes
And their murderous ways, wanted to change them
Into shrieking monkeys, but hesitated,
Grew uncertain, considered jackals instead,
Clucking hens, thinking perhaps a greasy rat
On the kitchen wall would suit the loudmouths better,
In fact, going from A to Z in the Bestiary
Without finding a single species to even approximate
The thieving sneaks with their lying tongues,
Not even among the shithouse flies and graveyard worms
Who are far more truthful and noble,
Make no mistake, in their conduct and in their grit.

THE BIG COVERUP

The world is full of amateur detectives
Working on unsolved crimes.
Their eyes and ears open when ours are closed.
The street of many concealed felonies
So pretty in the morning sunlight.

The crimes are ancient and the day is new.
To the gun on the table someone whispers,
You are beautiful.
Beast of the night, was that him?
He scratched on the door and asked to use the phone.
Ten years later he's still here,
Washing her dishes in the kitchen.

The sun shines. The chain of clues leads to
Some chickens living in a rusty old hearse
In your neighbor's backyard.
Their eggs' whiteness is positively sinister.
That same day the mailman confesses
He's engaged to a wealthy society woman
With whom he spent one wild night on the town.

Heavenly Justice, there is also that.
A monomaniacal tycoon with worldwide business
        interests
Who treats his employees like galley slaves
But who also likes to appear on occasion
As a shy little girl wearing her First Communion dress.
You get the picture?

EMPIRES

My grandmother prophesied the end
Of your empires, O fools!
She was ironing. The radio was on.
The earth trembled beneath our feet.

One of your heroes was giving a speech.
"Monster," she called him.
There were cheers and gun salutes for the monster.
"I could kill him with my bare hands,"
She announced to me.

There was no need to. They were all
Going to the devil any day now.
"Don't go blabbering about this to anyone,"
She warned me.
And pulled my ear to make sure I understood.

IN STRANGE CITIES

The way a curving street
Reveals with each step
A novel sight,
Perhaps a high window
Shuttered against
The late afternoon sun,

With someone rising from
A bed of illicit love
To throw it open
Just as you pass by,
Green shutters clattering
Behind your back,

The sunlight ahead of you
Golden like a lion
Escaped from the zoo,
And now rearing up
In all his terror
And royal splendor.

THE STORY OF THE CRUCIFIXION

In which the roles are played
By our dearest friends.
Their children are the beggars.
Their purebred dogs the Roman soldiers.

They are climbing a bare hill
On a windy day in spring.
The clouds are rushing ahead of them
As if to be there first.

A number of solitary figures
Stand apart waving their arms.
They all want the part
Of the long-suffering Saviour for themselves.

Windy day. A bare hill
Like the closely cropped head of a convict.
The dogs like Roman soldiers,
The children like swarming beggars.

MIDNIGHT SERENADERS

We are father and son,
Each taking turn
Whistling in the dark.
We are not very brave.
This is for you alone in bed
With the covers over your head.

A few piercing blue notes.
It's late and we are tired.
There was a wedding.
The bride and groom
Held each other close on the dance floor.
The guests screamed
As the hotel plunged into darkness.

It was like the wind
Between the cold winter stars.
A creaky door
Way out in the darkness.
Some kind of small bird
Trapped by a cat
And calling on heaven to witness.

AT SUNSET

O fly, frightened away
By sudden gunfire,
Crows are pecking excitedly in the road
Where you just rested.

Here's a city at sunset
Resembling a butcher's fresh carcass.
Here's the house of the Lord.
Open, cool, and empty.
He could be in throes of love
And sighing amorously
The way he twists his body on the cross.

Go and crawl into his empty eye sockets
And see what he sees.
The open door, the street at dusk,
A few children at play,
A dog looking over his shoulder,
The blind man tapping his cane.

ROMANTIC LANDSCAPE

To grieve, always to suffer
At the thought of time passing.
The outside world shadowy
As your deepest self.
Melancholy meadows, trees so still,
They seem afraid of themselves.

The sunset sky for one brief moment
Radiant with some supreme insight,
And then it's over. Tragic theater:
Blood and mourning at which
Even the birds fall silent.

Spirit, you who are everywhere and nowhere,
Watch over the lost lamb
Now that the mouth of the Infinite
Opens over us
And its dumb tongue begins to move darkly.

DARK TV SCREEN

The memory of this day's evil
Like a meat stall covered with flies.
Soul—flown through the open window.
Heart chewed like a dog's ball.

There's a boot lifted above us all
As in a children's book.
An army boot studded with nails,
While the ants down below scurry.

O Cordelia, my name is Lear. My name is
Primo Levi. I sit naked between
The open window and the dark TV screen,
My hands and sex bathed in the fire of evening.

PRAYER

You who know only the present moment,
O Lord,
You who remember nothing
Of what came before,
Who admire the beauty
Of a dead child,
The lovers embraced
In a field of yellow flowers.

The game of chess
And the cracks on the poorhouse wall
Are equally interesting
And incomprehensible to You
Who know what it's like to be a tiger,
A mouse in the instant of danger,
And know nothing of my regrets,
My solitudes,
And my infinite horror of You.

CHILDREN OF THE STORM

At daybreak, I heard the birds
Brag of their new loves
In the dark oak trees
Around my house.

And in that half-light
And sweet awakening,
I shivered under the blankets,
Naked as I was,
Remembering the way you used to rise early
With soft step,
Obscure purpose,

To stand at the open window,
Breathing the silence
With eyes raised
Watching the light's slow coming,
Coming to say,
You have been exceptionally favored
By a power magnificent and terrible.

MYSTICS

Help me to find what I've lost,
If it was ever, however briefly, mine,
You who may have found it.
Old man praying in the privy,
Lonely child drawing a secret room
And in it a stopped clock.

Seek to convey its truth to me
By hints and omens.
The room in shadow, perhaps the wrong room?
The cockroach on the wall,
The naked lovers kissing
On the TV with the sound off.
I could hear the red faucet drip.

Or else restore to plain view
What is eternally invisible
And speaks by being silent.
Blue distances to the North,
The fires of the evening to the West,
Christ himself in pain, panhandling
On the altar of the storefront church
With a long bloody nail in each palm.

In this moment of amazement . . .
Since I do ask for it humbly,
Without greed, out of true need.
My teeth chattered so loudly,
My old dog got up to see what's the matter.
Oh divine lassitude, long drawn-out sigh
As the vision came and went.

IMPORTED NOVELTIES

They didn't answer to repeated knocks,
Or perhaps they were in no hurry.
On the eighteenth floor
Even the sunlight moved lazily
Past the floating dust.
A year could pass here, I thought,
As in a desert solitude.

"Unknown parties, rarely seen,"
The elevator operator warned me.
He wore a New Year's party hat in August;
I was looking for work.

Inside, I imagined rows of file cabinets,
Old desks, dead telephones.
I could have been sitting at one of them myself,
Like someone doused with gasoline
In the moment before the match is lit,

But then the elevator took me down.

VIA DEL TRITONE

In Rome, on the street of that name,
I was walking alone in the sun
In the noonday heat, when I saw a house
With shutters closed, the sight of which
Pained me so much, I could have
Been born there and left inconsolably.

The ochre walls, the battered old door
I was tempted to push open and didn't,
Knowing already the coolness of the entrance,
The garden with a palm tree beyond,
And the dark stairs on the left.

Shutters closed to cool shadowy rooms
With impossibly high ceilings,
And here and there a watery mirror
And my pale and contorted face
To greet me and startle me again and again.

"You found what you were looking for,"
I expected someone to whisper.
But there was no one, neither there
Nor in the street, which was deserted
In that monstrous heat that gives birth
To false memories and tritons.

SHAVING

Child of sorrow.
Old snotnose.
Stray scrap from the table of the gods.
Toothless monkey.
Workhorse,
Wheezing there,
Coughing too.

The trouble with you is,
Your body and soul
Don't get along well together.
Pigsty for a brain,
Stop them from making faces at each other
In the mirror!
Then, remove the silly angel wings
From your gorilla suit.

TRAILER PARK

Lewis and Clark,
You never found anything
To compare.
Trees without leaves,
Naked branches,
And then a snowflake or two
In flight
From the darkening sky.

End of town,
No sign of life
In any of the trailers
As you drive by slowly,
The ground bare,
Frozen
This overcast morning
While he squats absorbed
In a game.

A small child bent over a toy
On a road to Calvary.
In the distance, the crows
Already perched
On crosses
Of unknown prophets
And thieves.

THE TOWER

Five, six chairs piled up in the yard
And you on top of them
Sitting like a hanging judge,
Wearing only pajama bottoms.

The sparrows, what must they think?
If people are watching,
They are as quiet as goldfish,
Or expensive cuts of meat.

Hour after hour alone with the sky
And its mad serenity
On the rickety, already teetering,
Already leaning tower.

How frightened the neighbors must be.
Not even a child walks the streets
In this heat,
Not even a car passes and slows down.

What do you see in the distance, O father?
A windowpane struck by the setting sun?
A game called on account of darkness?
The players like fleas in a convent.

Hell's bells about to toll?

LITTLE PROPHET

The beard of the little prophet
Curled out of the chimney into the sky.
"You'll need a huge comb today, father,"
We whispered in his ear
As he lay in bed with eyes closed.

"God is a circus master," he said.
"His only son is inside a lion's cage.
He wants everybody to come and see his son
Ride the young lioness
Wearing his wreath of thorns."

Caravans passed through his room.
Gypsies and dogs ate off his plate.
Then his beard escorted them across the sky.
"Goodbye little prophet," they shouted,
But he just lay there smiling at the ceiling.

MYSTERY WRITER

I figured, well, since I can't sleep
I'll go for a walk.
After the rain, being so late,
The streets must be deserted.
The dark shadows and my thoughts
Will keep me company.

As I expected, there was no one.
Wee-hour drifters, fellow insomniacs,
All those incapable of happiness,
Where were they all now?
I went roaming down blocks so poorly lit,
So vile and desolate,

I quickened my pace. Everything seemed
Anciently abandoned,
Closed forever and impervious to argument.
I wanted to see around the next corner,
And the next, and the next,
Beyond the last rusted car:

A painted woman in a doorway,
Elsewhere a knife drawn at me,
A storefront church with lights on,
Jesus ripped from the altar
Lying on the sidewalk,
His mouth open and silent.

Running now, unbuttoning my coat
With my ink-stained fingers.
Thinking, you are the mystery writer,
This night and this city
Are the work of your hands!
And I had no one specific in mind!

THE SECRET

I have my excuse, Mr. Death,
The old note my mother wrote
The day I missed school.
Snow fell. I told her my head hurt
And my chest. The clock struck
The hour. I lay in my father's bed
Pretending to be asleep.

Through the window I could see
The snow-covered roofs. In my mind
I rode a horse; I was in a ship
On a stormy sea. Then I dozed off.
When I woke, the house was still.
Where was my mother?
Had she written the note and left?

I rose and went searching for her.
In the kitchen our white cat sat
Picking at the bloody head of a fish.
In the bathroom the tub was full,
The mirror and the window fogged over.

When I wiped them, I saw my mother
In her red bathrobe and slippers
Talking to a soldier on the street
While the snow went on falling,
And she put a finger
To her lips, and held it there.

DATE DUE			

2/00

R0123294474   HUMCA   811
S589

HOUSTON PUBLIC LIBRARY
CENTRAL LIBRARY

4/10